Attainment's
Life Skill Readers

40 Topics Focus on Community Activities

Craig Booth
Judi Kinney

Win/Mac CD

This CD contains a printable PDF of the entire book. You can review and print pages from your computer. The PDF (portable document format) file requires Acrobat Reader software. If you have Acrobat Reader already on your computer, run the program and then open the file using LSRGuide.pdf from the CD.

To Install Acrobat Reader for Windows:
Run ARINSTALL.EXE provided on the CD. After installation, run Acrobat Reader; then open using LSRGuide.pdf

To install Acrobat Reader for Mac:
Run Reader Installer. After installation, open using LSRGuide.pdf

By Craig Booth and Judi Kinney
Edited by Tom Kinney
Graphic Design by Lynn Chrisman
Photography by Craig Booth and Beverly Potts
Cover Art by Jo Reynolds

ISBN: 1-57861-549-6

An Attainment Publication
©2005 Attainment Company, Inc.

Attainment Company, Inc.
P.O. Box 930160
Verona, Wisconsin 53593-0160
1-800-327-4269

www.AttainmentCompany.com

Life Skill Readers

Introduction

Life Skill Readers presents six color-coded, easy-to-read chapters, all of which are augmented with extensive use of photographs. Chapters include: Community, Personal, School, Signs, Transportation and Work. The book can be given directly to users to read, or you can print out the assigned pages from the PDF of the book which is on CD-ROM. A third option is to photocopy assigned pages of the book, which for this purpose is in a covered spiralbound format.

Forty topic areas run across the six chapters. Each area consists of a photographically illustrated story followed by study questions. All stories are either three, five or seven pages long. Throughout the book this presentation is standardized, with two blocks of vocabulary-controlled text per page and corresponding pictures above the text. All photographs are contemporary and realistic. Text blocks correspond to multiple photos which are there to reinforce the meaning of the text. The forty study questions pages follow a standard format.

Who is Life Skill Readers For?

The primary audiences for *Life Skill Readers* are adolescents and adults who read at a second grade level or below. Younger readers will also find most stories "age appropriate." Three approaches for students to use *Life Skill Readers* are listed below:

1. **Student reads independently.** Students independently read the stories and answer the study questions.
2. **Student reads with assistance.** Students read the stories with the encouragement and oversight of a tutor or instructor. When completing study questions, instructors can give hints to struggling students.
3. **Tutor reads story to student.** The student listens to the story being read by the instructor. The instructor encourages participation by repeatedly pointing to and discussing picture content. Study questions are read to the student who can answer verbally or with accommodations.

Additional Instructional Activities

In addition to the merging of life skill instruction with reading comprehension, there are several additional instructional activities you can incorporate:

1. Find examples of functional sight words in the text and compile corresponding vocabulary lists for each student. If you have time, you can also make individual sight word cards for independent study for each student.

Life Skill Readers

2. Link community outings to relevant topics, like "Grocery Stores," "Fast Food Restaurants" and "Visiting the Library" and discuss with students.
3. Give homework assignments by simply reproducing stories and lessons and sending them along with students at the end of the school day.

Aligning to Standards and IEP Objectives

Recent national trends toward setting high standards, which have emanated from No Child Left Behind and IDEA 2004, as well as local initiatives on the part of individual school districts have combined to energize literacy instruction for students with significant disabilities. In the process, there has been an increased emphasis on aligning instruction to standards through IEPs. Examples of appropriate standards could include:

1. Identifying themes from the text,
2. Responding to comprehension questions,
3. Retelling a story in sequence, and
4. Writing about reading materials.

Writing to Student IEPs

The areas of literacy and life skills are often addressed in student IEPs. *Life Skill Readers* makes a point of covering numerous daily living activities as well as community and vocational skill areas for transition students. Instructors will find that using the study questions to write measurable goals and objectives to student IEPs is very handy. Sample IEP objectives and benchmarks are included below:

Life Skill Objectives

1. Student will read and answer questions to a story.
   a. Will predict content based upon title, pictures or captions.

   b. Will read the story.
   c. Will locate information and answer the questions.

2. With prompts will read the story and answer questions.
   a. With prompts will predict content based upon title, pictures or captions.
   b. With prompts will read the story.
   c. With prompts will locate information and answer the questions.

3. Will listen to the story and answer the questions read.
   a. With prompts will predict content based upon title, pictures or captions.
   b. Will listen to the story.
   c. Will listen to and answer questions read.

Community

Community

Community

Personal

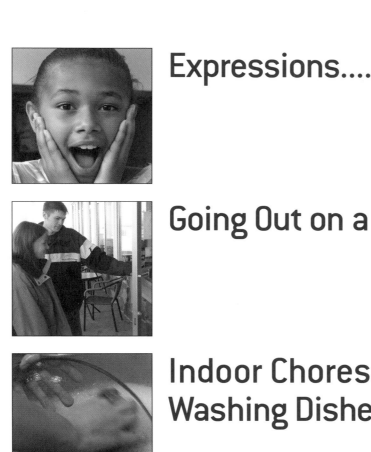

Personal

School

Signs

Transportation

Work

Barbershops 1

People go to barbershops to get their hair cut or styled.

The person who cuts your hair is called a barber.

Barbershops 2

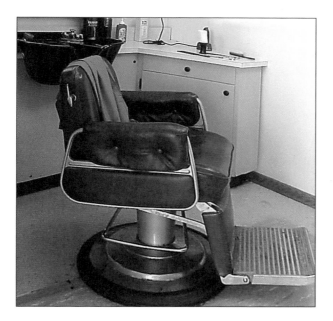 

When you get your hair cut you sit in a special chair that turns and moves up and down.

 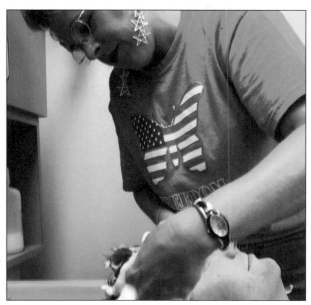

Some barbershops have sinks for washing hair.

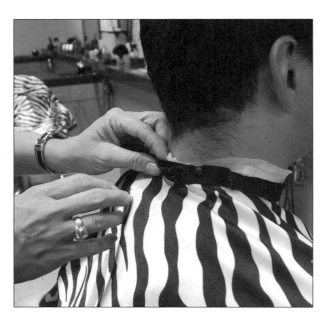

The barber wraps a sheet around your shoulders
so hair does not fall on your clothes.

Barbers use a comb and scissors to cut hair.

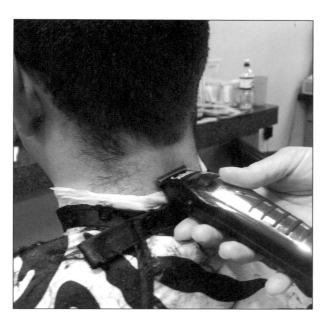

Sometimes they use an electric hair clipper.

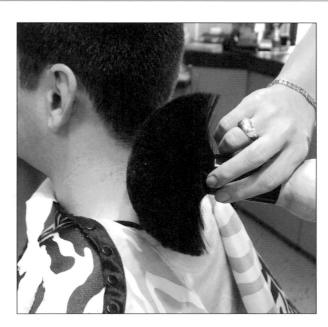

After the haircut, the barber brushes loose hair
from your face and neck.

The barber tells you how much to pay for the haircut.

You look good after you get your hair cut.

Study Questions Barbershops 6

Name _____ Date _____

Directions: Circle the answer.

1. People go to the barbershop to get:

    a. laundry washed.

    b. hair cut and styled.

    c. drinks and food.

2. Barbers use:

    a. books, magazines and CDs.

    b. drinks, food and desserts.

    c. combs, scissors and electric clippers.

Directions: Write the word to complete the sentence.

3. A person who cuts hair is called a _____.

    (barber)

Challenge: Answer.

4. How often do you go to a barber?

_____

5. Name something you can buy at the barbershop.

_____

Doors 1

Many large buildings have automatic doors that open before you touch them. Some doors open when you pull them sideways.

Do not play around automatic doors because you could get injured.

Doors 2

Some doors have buttons that people in wheelchairs can push to open automatically.

When you open a glass door use the handle to push it open.

Doors 3

It is important to know how to get out of buildings
if there is a fire.

Look for a door with a sign that says EXIT and go outside.
Most EXIT signs are bright red so you can see them easily.

Doors 4

Some doors are used only when there is an emergency.
If you open these doors you will hear an alarm.

Many buildings have revolving doors.

To use a revolving door, push on the door handle and keep walking until you get through.

It is important to know how to use different kinds of doors.

Study Questions **Doors** 6

Name _____ Date _____

Directions: Circle the answer.

1. Doors that open before you touch them are:

    a. revolving doors.

    b. manual doors.

    c. automatic doors.

2. Doors that have alarms on them are:

    a. automatic doors.

    b. emergency doors.

    c. revolving doors.

Directions: Write the word to complete the sentence.

3. To go out of a building, look for a sign that says _____.

                                                      (EXIT)

Challenge: Answer.

4. What is a safety tip about automatic doors?

_____

5. What kind of door does your school have?

_____

Fast Food Restaurants 1

At a fast food restaurant, your food is ready for you as soon as you order it.

A menu board behind the counter shows prices of food you can order.

Cashiers type your order on a computer and tell you how much to pay.

Then the cashier puts your food on a tray.

 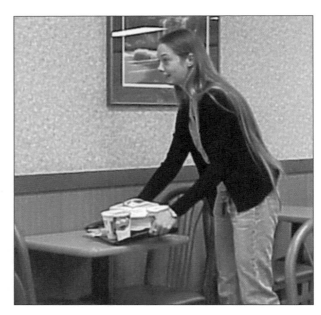

After paying for your meal, you take the tray and find a place to sit.

Some fast food restaurants let you pour your own drink.

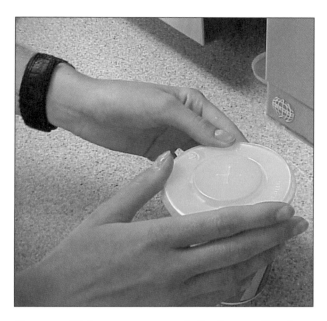 

Put a lid on your drink so it does not spill and use a straw to drink it.

Use napkins when you eat. Some restaurants put napkin holders on every table.

When you are done eating, empty your tray and put it on top of the trash bin.

Fast food restaurants are good places to eat when you are in a hurry.

Study Questions
Fast Food Restaurants 6

Name _____ Date _____

Directions: Circle the answer.

1. A menu board:

    a. shows prices of food.

    b. shows prices of rooms.

    c. shows prices of tickets.

2. What does the cashier at a fast food restaurant do?

    a. combs and cuts hair.

    b. gives you a key to a room.

    c. puts food on a tray and takes your money.

Directions: Write the word to complete the sentence.

3. Use a _____ when you eat.

                    (napkin)

Challenge: Answer.

4. When is a fast food restaurant a good place to eat?

_____

5. What is your favorite fast food restaurant?

_____

Fire Departments 1

Fire departments are an important part of every community.

Fire trucks rush to emergencies. Loud sirens and flashing lights alert people to get out of their way.

Firefighters use long ladders and hoses to spray water on fires.

Firefighters rescue people if they are hurt or in danger.

Being a firefighter is a dangerous job.

They have to do a lot of training before they can start their job.

They wear heavy uniforms and carry oxygen tanks on their backs to protect them when they fight fires.

Firefighters can be your friends, neighbors or relatives.

If you are near a fire or an accident, leave or stand far away so the firefighters can do their job.

Study Questions **Fire Departments** 6

Name _____ Date _____

Directions: Circle the answer.

1. A person who puts out fires is called a:

    a. barber.

    b. firefighter.

    c. policeman.

2. Firefighters use:

    a. long ladders and hoses.

    b. cash registers and trays.

    c. tractors and silos.

Directions: Write the word to complete the sentence.

3. Firefighters wear heavy _____ .

                                                (uniforms)

Challenge: Answer.

4. Why is it important to stand away from a fire?

_____

5. Write one thing a firefighter does.

_____

Grocery stores are an important part of the community.
People shop in them for food to take home.

Make a grocery list before you go shopping.
The list should include all the items you need to buy.

Grocery Stores 2

Use a shopping cart or basket when shopping.
They help you carry your groceries.

Grocery stores have products on shelves on both sides
of the aisles.

Grocery Stores 3

Walk down the aisles to look for items on your grocery list.

When you find items you are looking for, put them in your cart or basket.

Grocery Stores 4

Some products are found in special sections. The dairy section has products like milk, cheese and butter.

The meat department has products like pork, beef, chicken and turkey.

Some products are kept in the frozen food section.
The big freezers keep food cold so it doesn't spoil.

Fresh fruits and vegetables are found in the produce section.

When you are done, take your basket or cart to the checkout line. The clerk scans the products you selected and tells you how much you owe.

Most stores put your groceries in bags so they are easy to take home.

Some people pay for their groceries with cash.
Others write checks or use credit cards.

Grocery stores are important because they sell food
we eat everyday.

Study Questions **Grocery Stores** 8

Name _____ Date _____

Directions: Circle the answer.

1. The dairy section of a grocery store has:

    a. pork, beef and chicken.

    b. fruits and vegetables.

    c. milk, cheese and butter.

2. The produce section of a grocery store has:

    a. frozen foods.

    b. fruits and vegetables.

    c. milk, cheese and butter.

Directions: Write the word to complete the sentence.

3. Freezers keep food _____ .

                                                     (cold)

Challenge: Answer.

4. Make a list of three things you can buy at a grocery store.

    a. _____

    b. _____

    c. _____

5. Name two ways you can pay at a grocery store.

    a. _____

    b. _____

Hardware Stores 1

A hardware store sells many items to use in and around your house.

 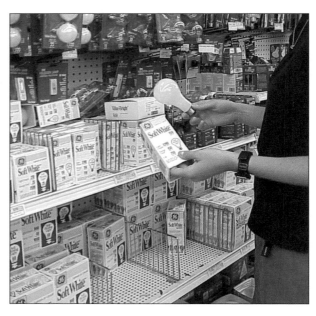

Light bulbs come in many different sizes and wattages.

Make sure you know what kind of light bulbs you need before you purchase them.

Tools are helpful when making or repairing things around your home.

Many kitchen items can also be found at a hardware store. Small appliances, like electric can openers and toaster ovens, allow you to quickly prepare food.

Items in the Lawn and Garden section change by season.

For example, there are rakes and lawn mowers in the summer, and snow blowers and shovels in the winter

Paint comes in many different colors. If you cannot find the right color, a store clerk can mix the exact color for you.

Many kitchen items can also be found at a hardware store.
Small appliances, like electric can openers and toaster ovens,
allow you to quickly prepare food.

Whether you are building, fixing, or looking for something new to use
in your house, you should be able to find it at a hardware store.

Study Questions **Hardware Stores** 6

Name _____ Date _____

Directions: Circle the answer.

1. A hardware store sells:

     a. many items to eat.

     b. many items to wear.

     c. many items to use in a home.

2. Some items found in a hardware store are:

     a. dairy products, meat and produce.

     b. tools, rakes and paint.

     c. clothes, shoes and coats.

Directions: Write the word to complete the sentence.

3. Small appliances can be found in a _____ store.

                                              (hardware)

Challenge: Answer.

4. Make a list of three items you can buy in a hardware store.

     a. _____

     b. _____

     c. _____

5. Write one reason why you would go to a hardware store.

     _____

Hotels 1

Hotels are a place for people to stay when they are away from home.

When you stay at a hotel you must first check in at the front desk.

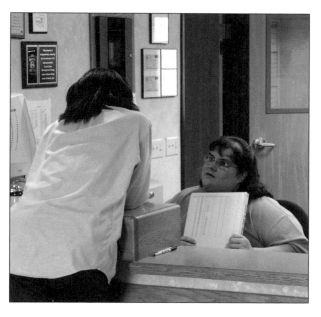 

A desk clerk will give you a key to unlock the door to your room.

Use the key to unlock the door to your room.

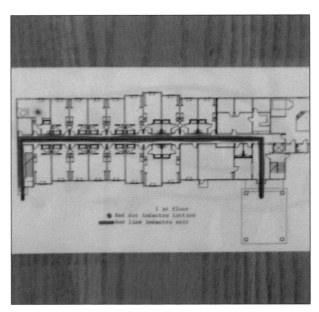

The back of the door has important information.
Signs show you the fastest way to get out of the hotel in
case of an emergency.

Hotels provide you with almost everything you could find in
your own house.

Some hotels have swimming pools for their guests to use.

If you get hungry, some hotels have their own restaurants.

When you are away from home, hotels are a good place to spend the night.

Study Questions **Hotels** 6

Name _____ Date _____

Directions: Circle the answer.

1. Hotels are places to stay when:

    a. you want a haircut.

    b. you are away from home.

    c. you want to see a video.

2. What is one thing a hotel clerk does?

    a. scans your items.

    b. puts food on a tray.

    c. gives you a key to your room.

Directions: Write the word to complete the sentence.

3. On the back of the door is a sign for what to do in an

_____.

(emergency)

Challenge: Answer.

4. When did you stay in a hotel?

_____

5. Tell one thing you did at the hotel.

_____

Laundromats 1

A laundromat is a place you can go to wash dirty clothes.

Laundromats have vending machines that sell everything you need to wash clothes, like laundry soap and fabric softener.

Laundromats 2

Rows of washing machines and clothes dryers are found in the laundromat.

Check the front of the machines to see how much money is needed and then insert the correct amount of coins to operate them.

Laundromats 3

Laundry carts are useful for carrying laundry.
They have wheels that make them easy to move around.

Most laundromats have a place for you to sit while you wait
for your laundry to finish.

Laundromats 4

Sometimes there are magazines you can read.

Tables are used for folding and sorting clothes. Make sure to do this before taking them home.

Laundromats 5

Laundromats are an important part of the community because they provide a place for people to wash their laundry.

Study Questions **Laundromats** 6

Name _____ Date _____

Directions: Circle the answer.

1. Laundromats have vending machines that sell

    a. laundry soap and fabric softener.

    b. newspapers.

    c. hamburgers and sandwiches.

2. What can you find in a Laundromat?

    a. aisles with items on both sides.

    b. washing machines, dryers and laundry carts.

    c. tools, rakes and paint.

Directions: Write the word to complete the sentence.

3. _____ are used for folding clothes.

      (Tables)

Challenge: Answer.

4. Why do people go to a Laundromat?

_____

Circle yes or no.

5. Have you ever been to a Laundromat?

      yes   no

Libraries 1

The public library is a place to go to read books and magazines, research on the internet, listen to records or CDs or check out videos.

Find books by typing in the titles or authors on the computerized card catalog. If you don't know how to do it, ask the staff for help.

Libraries 2

Library books are organized into fiction and non-fiction.

The fiction section is arranged by author, and non-fiction by subject.

Libraries 3

There is a separate area with books just for children.

A librarian checks out the books for you to take home and lets you know when to bring them back.

Libraries 4

Drop off books in the book depository slot when you bring them back to the library.

Libraries are a good place to find information.
Look for a library near where you live.

Libraries 5

Libraries are quiet places to learn more about any subject that interests you.

Study Questions **Libraries** 6

Name _____ Date _____

Directions: Circle the answer.

1. In a library you can find books by using:

    a. a menu.

    b. a computerized card catalog.

    c. a recipe.

2. Library books are organized by:

    a. small appliances and tools.

    b. meat and dairy products.

    c. fiction and non-fiction.

Directions: Write the word to complete the sentence.

3. A _____ checks out your books.

           (librarian)

Challenge: Answer.

4. List three things you can find in a library.

    a. _____

    b. _____

    c. _____

5. What was the last book you checked out of a library?

_____

Restaurants 1

People eat at restaurants everyday.

Most restaurants look different from the outside.

Restaurants 2

Some restaurants look the same and serve the same food wherever you go.

Wait staff serve you at sit down restaurants.

Restaurants 3

They take your order and bring food to your table.

At fast food restaurants you order your food at a counter and use a tray to carry it to your table.

Restaurants 4

Some fast food restaurants have drive-through windows so you can order food without getting out of your car.

Some restaurants sell only certain foods like Mexican, Chinese, seafood, sandwiches or ice cream.

Whatever you like to eat, you can always find restaurants near you with good food.

Study Questions **Restaurants** 6

Name _____ Date _____

Directions: Circle the answer.

1. Wait staff serve you at what kind of restaurant?

    a. sit down restaurant.

    b. fast food restaurant.

    c. drive-through windows.

2. You order food at a counter when you go to a:

    a. sit down restaurant.

    b. fast food restaurant.

    c. drive-through window.

Directions: Write the word to complete the sentence.

3. Some fast food restaurants have a _____ -through window.

(drive)

Challenge: Answer.

4. What is your favorite restaurant?

_____

5. What do you like to order when you go to a restaurant?

_____

People go to sit down restaurants to eat with friends and family.

You must wait for the host or hostess to show you to a table at a sit down restaurant.

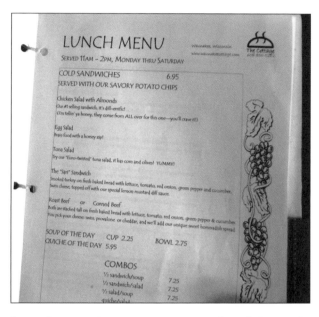

Look at the menu to decide what to eat. Menus have special sections for drinks, food and desserts.

The wait staff will come to your table to take your order.

Some restaurants have salad bars where you can make your own salad.

The wait staff brings your food to the table when it's ready.

Sit Down Restaurants 4

When you are done eating, the wait staff will give you a bill. The bill tells you how much you owe.

At some restaurants you can pay the wait staff at your table. At others you take the bill to the front counter and pay the cashier.

At sit down restaurants, leave a tip on your table before you go. A tip thanks the wait staff for good service.

A sit down restaurant is a good place to eat when you have time to enjoy your meal.

Study Questions
Sit Down Restaurants 6

Name _____ Date _____

Directions: Circle the answer.

1. What does the host or hostess do at a sit down restaurant?

    a. puts food on a tray.

    b. scans your food.

    c. shows you to a table.

2. The wait staff at a sit down restaurant:

    a. takes your order and brings you the food.

    b. takes your order and puts your food on a tray.

    c. scans your food and puts it into a bag.

Directions: Write the word to complete the sentence.

3. A way to thank the wait staff is to give a _____ .

                                        (tip)

Challenge: Answer.

4. What is your favorite sit down restaurant?

_____

5. What do you like to order when you go to the restaurant?

_____

People go up or down in buildings by using stairs.

Some large buildings and shopping malls have escalators.
Escalators are automatic stairs.

You stand on the first step and they move up or down so you do not have to walk.

Elevators can also take people from one floor of a building to another. People in wheelchairs can use elevators.

Stairs, Escalators, and Elevators 3

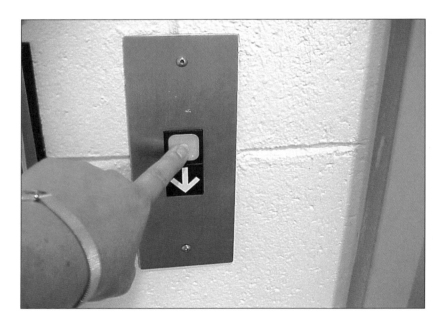

To use the elevator push the up button to go up or the down button to go down.

Wait until the right elevator arrives. If you are going up the up light will go on and the bell will ring when it arrives.

When the elevator doors open, walk inside. Push the button for the floor you want to go to and wait for the doors to close.

The elevator moves up or down to the right floor and then opens the doors for you to get out. Make sure the elevator has stopped at the right floor before you get out.

Never run or play near stairs, escalators or elevators.

Study Questions
Stairs, Escalators, and Elevators 6

Name _____ Date _____

Directions: Circle the answer.

1. Escalators are stairs that:

    a. you climb.

    b. are used by people in wheelchairs.

    c. are automatic.

2. To open an elevator door you need to:

    a. push the up or down button.

    b. step onto moving stairs.

    c. push the door that says: "stairs."

Directions: Write the word to complete the sentence.

3. When in an elevator you need to push the floor _____ .

                                                            (button)

Challenge: Answer.

4. Write one safety rule for using stairs, escalates or elevators.

_____

5. Name a place where there is an elevator.

_____

Stores 1

 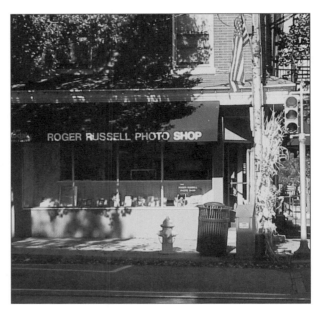

Stores are places that sell products to people.

Some stores sell a wide variety of products.

Stores 2

Other stores only sell certain products, like auto parts, movies or art supplies.

Some stores are in shopping malls. A mall is where different stores are together in one building.

Some stores have carts or baskets to help shoppers carry the items they want to buy.

Store signs show where to find products.

Sometimes signs tell the prices of items and let you know when items are on sale.

Stores have cash registers and clerks.

Clerks add prices of all products you buy and tell you how much to pay.

Some stores sell many different things and others sell only special items.

Study Questions **Stores** 6

Name _____ Date _____

Directions: Circle the answer.

1. A mall is a large building with many:

    a. small appliances.

    b. books to check out.

    c. different stores inside.

2. What do some stores have for customers?

    a. basket and carts to put items in.

    b. animals and farm machines.

    c. detergent and fabric softener.

Directions: Write the word to complete the sentence.

3. Signs with prices on them, tell what is on _____ .

                                                      (sale)

Challenge: Answer.

4. What is your favorite store to shop?

_____

5. Name the person who tells you how much to pay.

_____

On a farm you can find many kinds of animals, farm machines and buildings.

Many farms raise animals for food.

The farms produce food we eat and drink everyday.

Large tractors pull different types of machines through the fields to plant and harvest the food.

Tall silos store grains and other foods harvested for the animals on the farm.

Cows graze in pastures.

Eating grass helps them produce the milk we drink.

Big barns provide shelter for animals and a place to store tractors and other machinery.

Trip to the Farm 5

Farms are very important because they provide much of our food, like grains, dairy products, meat and poultry that we eat everyday.

Study Questions Trip to the Farm 6

Name _____ Date _____

Directions: Circle the answer.

1. Where is the food we eat and drink produced?

   a. a store.

   b. a farm.

   c. a restaurant.

2. Eating grass helps cows to:

   a. make milk.

   b. make food.

   c. make juice.

Directions: Write the word to complete the sentence.

_____ provide shelter for animals and machines.

    (Barns)

Challenge: Answer.

4. List three things you can find on a farm.

   a. _____

   b. _____

   c. _____

5. Have you ever been to a farm?

     yes   no

Trip to the Zoo 1

The zoo is a fun place to visit.

At the zoo you can watch and learn about different animals.

Polar bears live near the North Pole. Thick fur keeps them warm when it's cold outside. Polar bears have big, sharp paws.

Flamingos are pink birds with long legs. They eat tiny plants that grow in water, insects and small fish.

The biggest cat in the world is the tiger. Tigers hunt other animals for food. Their fur has black and brown stripes.

The Petting Zoo is a special area where you can touch and feed the animals.

Trip to the Zoo 4

Zoos also feature water mammals like seals, and animals from other continents like African zebras.

Larger animals like bears are exciting to see in zoos.

It is fun to spend a day at the zoo. Zoos have many different animals from around the world that you cannot see everyday.

Study Questions Trip to the Zoo 6

Name _____ Date _____

Directions: Circle the answer.

1. A zoo has many different

    a. cows.

    b. people.

    c. animals.

2. What is the biggest cat in the world?

    a. flamingo.

    b. polar bear.

    c. tiger.

Directions: Write the word to complete the sentence.

3. You can touch and feed animals in a Petting _____ .

    (Zoo)

Challenge: Answer.

4. What is your favorite zoo?

_____

5. What is your favorite zoo animal?

_____

Expressions 1

People can tell how you are feeling by looking at your face.

A smile shows that you are happy.

Expressions 2

 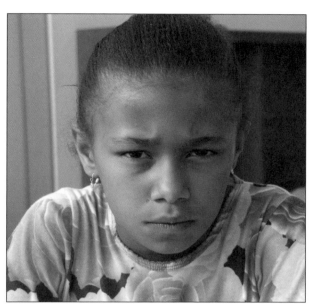

When you are angry, your eyebrows lower and lips tighten up.

People know you are sad when you do not smile and your face is turned down.

Expressions 3

When you are scared, your eyes and mouth open wide.
Sometimes you try to hide your face and eyes with your hands.

People have many expressions that show how they are feeling.
Can you think of some other expressions?

Study Questions **Expressions 4**

Name _____ Date _____

Directions: Circle the answer.

1. Expressions help people tell how you

    a. shop.

    b. feel.

    c. eat.

2. What happens when you are angry?

    a. Your mouth turns up.

    b. Your lips tighten.

    c. Your eyes are wide open.

Directions: Write the word to complete the sentence.

3. Expressions show how you _____ .

                                        (feel)

Challenge: Answer.

4. Write three expressions people show.

    a. _____

    b. _____

    c. _____

5. What makes you happy?

_____

When going out on a date, follow these tips to make the date more enjoyable. Take a shower and brush your teeth before you go. Dress appropriately for the date.

Be on time. It helps to wear a watch to keep track of the time.

Decide where and when you are going ahead of time.

If you have plans about what to do and where to go, you will have more fun.

Be polite to your date and other people around you. Talk with a normal voice and listen when your date is talking. Be yourself. You do not need to show off or behave differently.

Following these tips will make your date fun and enjoyable.

Study Questions
Going Out on a Date 4

Name _____ Date _____

Directions: Circle the answer.

1. What are some tips to do before going on a date?

    a. shower and brush your teeth.

    b. check out and see a movie.

    c. be late and don't call.

2. Why is it important to make a plan for a date?

    a. you will have more fun.

    b. you will spend more money.

    c. you will waste more time.

Directions: Write the word to complete the sentence.

3. It is important to be _____.

                                                    (polite)

Challenge: Answer.

4. Write three tips for dating.

    a. _____

    b. _____

    c. _____

5. Where would you go on a date?

_____

When you are finished with a meal, there are many dishes to be washed.

Use hot water and dish soap when filling the sink, but be careful not to burn yourself.

Check the water with your hand to make sure it is not too hot.

Use a sponge or dish rag to scrub the dishes until they are clean and then rinse them in fresh water with no soap in it.

Handle glass dishes gently so they do not break.

Be careful when washing sharp knives.

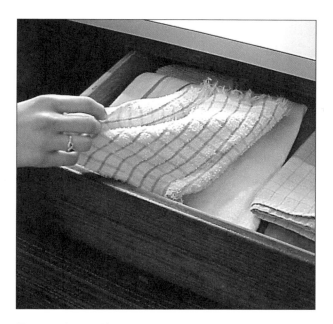 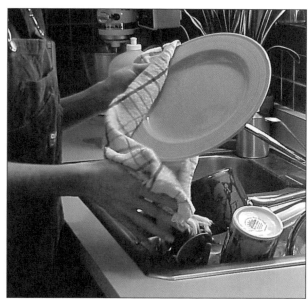

Dry the dishes using a clean, dry towel.

Put plates and glasses back where they belong.

Sort the silverware when putting it away.

It is important to do a good job washing dishes to remove germs that can make you sick.

Study Questions
Indoor Chores—Washing Dishes 6

Name _____ Date _____

Directions: Circle the answer.

1. What do you need to clean dishes?

    a. laundry detergent and fabric softener.

    b. a shower and brushed teeth.

    c. hot water and dish soap.

2. To scrub the dishes use:

    a. scrub brush or mop.

    b. sponge or dishrag.

    c. vacuum or dust rag.

Directions: Write the word to complete the sentence.

3. Dry dishes using a clean _____.

(towel)

Challenge: Answer.

4. Write one safety rule for doing the dishes.

_____

5. What chores do you do at home?

    a. _____

    b. _____

Outdoor Chores—Lawn Care 1

There are always chores to do outside.

One chore is mowing the grass. Never use a lawn mower without permission from an adult because they can be dangerous.

Always wear shoes, long pants, and eye protection to protect you from things you might hit when mowing.

Keep both hands on the handle and do not put hands or feet near the mower blade until it has stopped moving.

Use a rake to put leaves or grass into piles so it is easier to pick them up. When raking, wear gloves to prevent blisters on your hands.

Helping with outdoor chores is fun but you always need to be careful.

Study Questions
Outdoor Chores—Lawn Care 4

Name _____ Date _____

Directions: Circle the answer.

1. When mowing the lawn it is best to wear:

    a. sandals shorts and a t-shirt.

    b. coat, gloves and a hat.

    c. shoes, long pants and eye protection.

2. What is a safety tip for mowing the lawn?

    a. put glass and plastic in separate containers.

    b. keep away from a moving blade.

    c. wash hands before mowing the lawn.

Directions: Write the word to complete the sentence.

3. When raking wear _____ .

    (gloves)

Challenge: Answer.

4. Write one safety tip for outdoor chores.

_____

5. What outdoor chore do you do?

_____

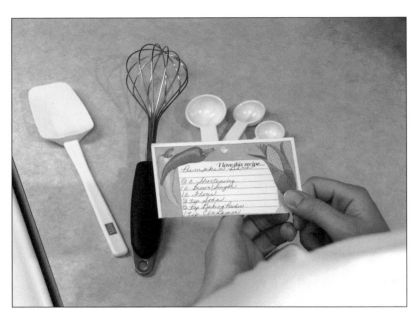

Making your own meal is a fun and rewarding experience.

Look at the recipe to make sure you have all the ingredients and tools you need.

Wash your hands and the work area with soap and water so you don't spread germs.

Be careful when using knives and other sharp utensils.

Preparing a Meal 3

Use potholders when you need to pick up hot pans or dishes.

Follow instructions on the recipe and measure the ingredients carefully.

When the food is done cooking, turn off the oven and stove burners.

Clean up your work area and wash all cooking utensils with dish soap.

When you are done, wash your hands again.

Name _____ Date _____

Directions: Circle the answer.

1. What do you need to do before making a meal?

    a. wear shoes and pants.

    b. shower and brush teeth.

    c. read the recipe and wash hands.

2. One safety tip to follow is:

    a. stay away from a moving blade.

    b. use potholders for hot pans.

    c. take out the trash.

Directions: Write the word to complete the sentence.

3. When making a meal use a _____ .

                                                                 (recipe)

Challenge: Answer.

4. Tell one thing to do after the meal is cooked.

_____

5. What do you like to cook?

_____

Some stores rent movies that you can watch at home.

To help you find the movies you want, rental stores organize them into categories like Westerns, Drama, Action, and Comedies.

When you find the movies you like, take them to the checkout counter and give the clerk your member card.

The clerk scans each movie and tells you what to pay and when you have to bring the movies back.

After you watch the movies, take them back to the video store. Take them inside and drop the movies in a special slot for movie returns.

Watching movies at home is a fun way to spend an evening alone or with friends.

Study Questions **Renting a Movie 4**

Name _____ Date _____

Directions: Circle the answer.

1. In movie rental stores, how are the movies organized?

    a. Westerns, Drama, Action and Comedies.

    b. fiction and non-fiction.

    c. tools and paints.

2. To check out a movie you need:

    a. a cart.

    b. a menu.

    c. a member card.

Directions: Write the word to complete the sentence.

3. The clerk scans the _____ .

    (movie)

Challenge: Answer.

4. What kind of movie do you like?

    _____

5. What is your favorite movie?

    _____

Taking Care of Pets 1

Taking care of a pet is a big responsibility. Pets need food and fresh water. Check their food and water everyday.

Some pets need daily exercise to stay healthy. Take them for a walk or to a park where they can run around.

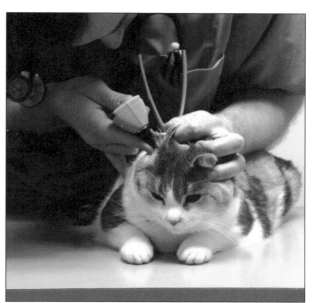

If your pet is ill, take it to a veterinarian. A veterinarian is a person who treats sick animals.

Some pets, like cats and dogs, need to wear a license. The license says who the pet belongs to if it gets lost.

Some pets need lots of attention. Spend a lot time with your pet to build a strong relationship.

Taking care of a pet requires a lot of responsibility but is a lot of fun.

Study Questions
Taking Care of Pets 4

Name _____ Date _____

Directions: Circle the answer.

1. What do pets need everyday?

    a. hair washed and cut.

    b. food and water.

    c. soap and fabric softener.

2. A person who cares for sick pets is a:

    a. veterinarian.

    b. librarian.

    c. firefighter.

Directions: Write the word to complete the sentence.

3. Some pets wear a _____.

                                    (license)

Challenge: Answer.

4. What pets do you have?

_____

5. How do you care for your pets?

_____

Everyone makes garbage. Leftover scraps of food, empty milk cartons, and old newspapers are all garbage.

Garbage should be placed in special containers to keep your community clean. This is called recycling.

Recycling means some garbage can be saved to use again.

Aluminum cans, glass bottles, and paper can all be recycled.

They should be separated from the garbage and put into separate containers.

When garbage containers are full at schools and businesses, janitors empty the trash and the recycle containers into dumpsters.

At home the garbage must be bagged up and set on the curb.

Recycled items are kept separate.

Garbage trucks collect the garbage and recyclables from homes and businesses and haul them away.

It is everyone's job to put trash where it belongs and recycle.

Study Questions
Recycling and Garbage 6

Name _____ Date _____

Directions: Circle the answer.

1. What does recycling mean?

    a. mowing the lawn.

    b. washing clothes.

    c. saving garbage to use again.

2. Items to recycle are:

    a. washed and put away.

    b. kept in separate containers.

    c. thrown away for good.

Directions: Write the word to complete the sentence.

3. _____ trucks collect recyclables.

    (Garbage)

Challenge: Answer.

4. List three things that can be recycled.

    a. _____

    b. _____

    c. _____

5. What does your school recycle?

    a. _____

    b. _____

    c. _____

Visit to the Dentist's Office 1

Most dentists send a card to remind you of regular checkups.
Go to your checkups to make sure you do not have cavities.

Dentist's offices have waiting rooms for you to sit in until they
are ready to see you.

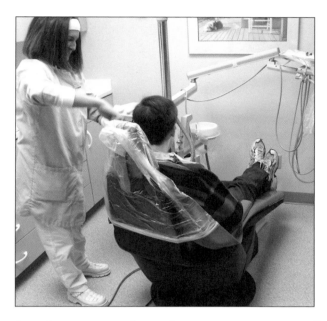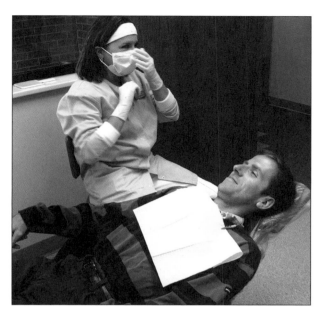

In the examination room you sit in a chair that leans way back so the dentist can see all of your teeth.

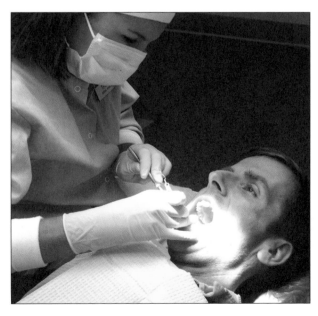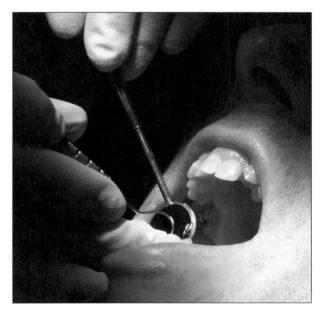

There are many tools a dentist uses to check and clean your teeth.

Visit to the Dentist's Office 3

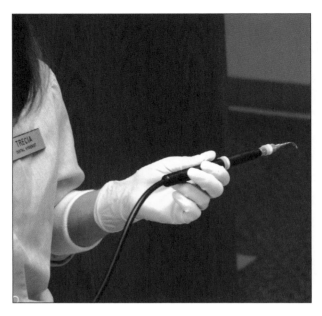 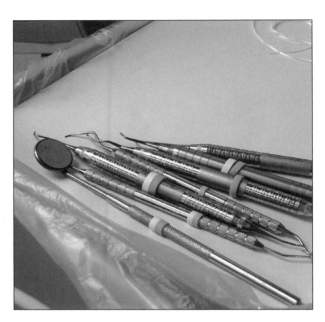

Some of tools a dentist uses are very sharp.

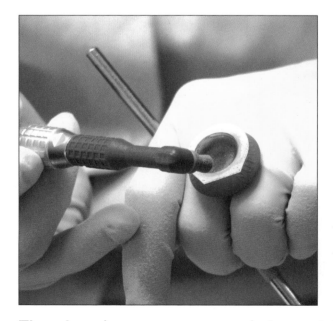 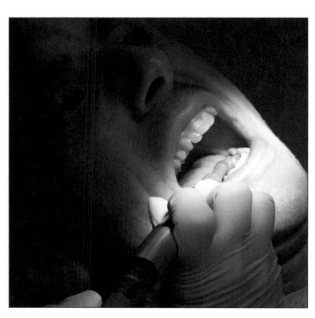

The dentist uses a special toothbrush and toothpaste.

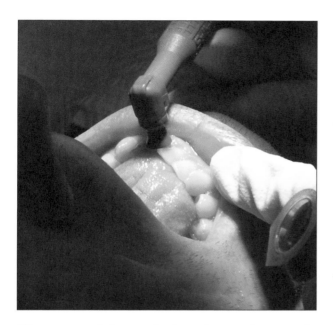
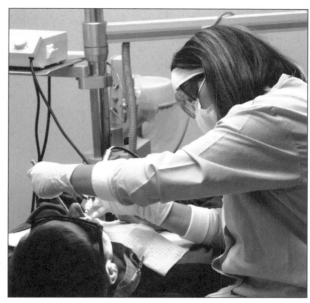

The toothbrush is electric and spins fast as it cleans your teeth.

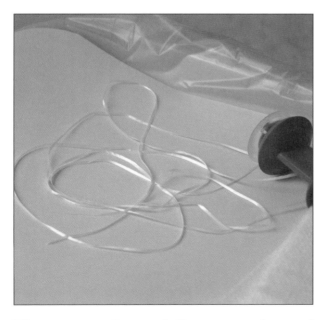
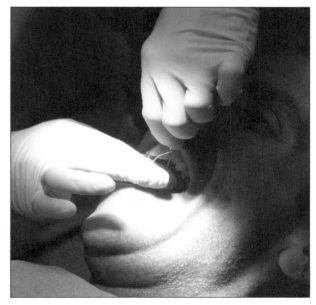

They use dental floss to clean between your teeth where the toothbrush cannot reach.

When the dentist is done you have a bright clean smile.

Study Questions
Visit to the Dentist's Office 6

Name _____ Date _____

Directions: Circle the answer.

1. Why do you go to a dentist?

   a. to clean and check your teeth.

   b. to get a check up or when you are sick.

   c. to get a haircut and style.

2. Some tools dentist use are:

   a. ladder and hose.

   b. stethoscope and blood pressure cup.

   c. special toothbrush and paste.

Directions: Write the word to complete the sentence.

3. To clean between your teeth, use _____.

   (floss)

Challenge: Answer.

4. Why is it important to go to a dentist?

   _____

5. How does a dentist remind you about your check-up?

   _____

Go to the doctor for regular checkups or when you feel sick. Before you see the doctor, check in at the registration desk.

Sit in the waiting room until your name is called. Usually, there are magazines to read while you wait.

The nurse will take you to an examination room.

Do not touch any of the tools while you wait for the doctor.

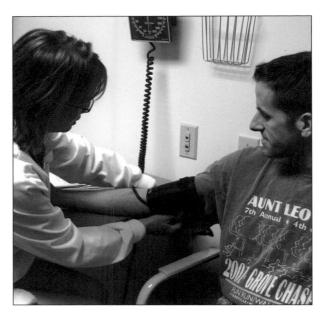

The nurse will record your weight and height, take your pulse, and measure your blood pressure.

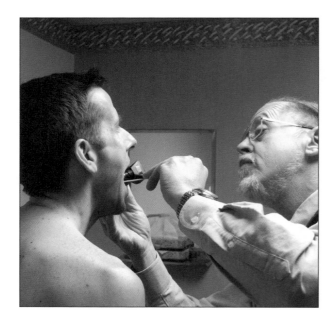
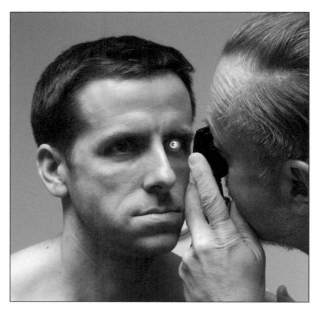

Then, the doctor will examine you, checking your ears, eyes, and throat.

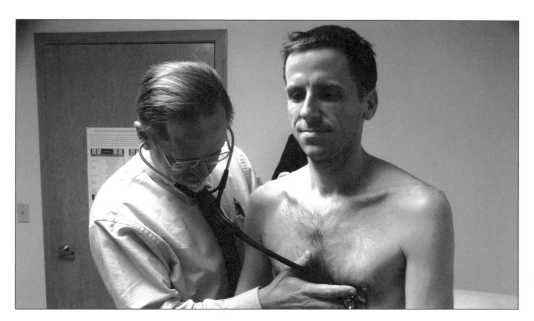

The doctor will listen to your heartbeat with a stethoscope.

If you are sick, the doctor will tell you what to do to get healthy, and may give you medicine if you need it.

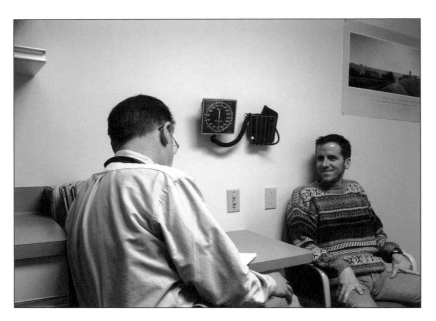

It is important to see a doctor when you are sick so that you can get better.

Study Questions
Visit to the Doctor's Office 6

Name _____ Date _____

Directions: Circle the answer.

1. Why do you go to a doctor's office?

    a. to clean and check your teeth.

    b. to get a check up or when you are sick.

    c. to get a haircut and styling.

2. What does a nurse do when you visit the doctor?

    a. record your weight and blood pressure.

    b. check your teeth.

    c. wash your hands.

Directions: Write the word to complete the sentence.

3. The doctor gives you _____ if you are sick.

                                         (medicine)

Challenge: Answer.

4. List three things a doctor does.

    a. _____

    b. _____

    c. _____

5. Why is it important to see a doctor when you are sick?

_____

Set the alarm early in the morning on school days, because you have a lot to do before you are ready to go.

 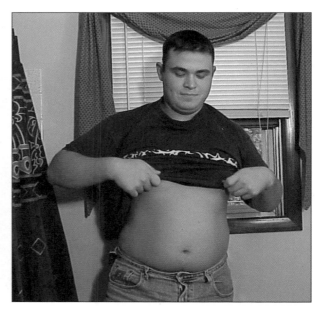

You have to brush your teeth, take a shower, use deodorant and mouthwash and get dressed in clean clothes.

Breakfast is the most important meal of the day. Make sure you have something to eat before you leave or you will run out of energy before lunch.

Most students use backpacks to carry books and school materials.

Before leaving for school, remember to check yourself over. Make sure you have everything you need for the day in your backpack.

Follow these same steps everyday to help you remember all the things you need to do when getting ready for school.

Study Questions
Getting Ready for School 4

Name _____ Date _____

Directions: Circle the answer.

1. What do you need to do before going to school?

   a. get your hair cut and styled.

   b. shower and use deodorant.

   c. use warm water and dish soap.

2. What is the most important meal of the day?

   a. breakfast.

   b. lunch.

   c. dinner.

Directions: Write the word to finish the sentence.

3. Before going to school check yourself and your _____.

   (backpack)

Challenge: Answer.

4. What time do you get up before school?

_____

5. List three things you do to get ready for school.

   a. _____

   b. _____

   c. _____

Riding the School Bus 1

The school bus is one way to get to and from school. You need to follow certain rules when riding the bus.

Stand back from the road while waiting for the bus.

If others are waiting with you, keep your hands to yourself. Keep some space between you and the other kids.

Form a line when the bus arrives and wait for the driver to open the bus door.

Find a place to sit down and face the front of the bus. If it has seatbelts, put them on.

Talk quietly to your neighbors and listen to the bus driver in case there are special instructions.

Stay in your seats until the bus stops at the drop off area.

Gather your belongings and stand up in the aisle. Do not push or shove others waiting in front of you.

Step carefully off the bus and walk to the designated area until school starts.

Following these rules will make your bus ride fun and safe.

Study Questions
Riding the Schoolbus 6

Name _____ Date _____

Directions: Circle the answer.

1. What are some rules to follow when you wait for a school bus?

    a. use deodorant and put on clean clothes.

    b. walk quietly into the school and go to your locker.

    c. stand back from the road and keep your hands to yourself.

2. What are some rules to follow when riding a school bus?

    a. Stay in your seat and talk quietly.

    b. Hang up your backpack and get out your homework.

    c. Carry your tray and sit down at a table.

Directions: Write the word to complete the sentence.

3. The person who drives the bus is the bus _____.

    (driver)

Challenge: Answer.

4. How do you get to school?

_____

5. What are two rules to follow when riding your school bus?

    a. _____

    b. _____

Starting School in the Morning 1

After you arrive at school, you might have to wait outside before school starts. Stay in the designated areas until the bell rings.

After the bell rings, enter the school quietly and walk to your locker or coat rack.

Hang up your backpack and your coat or jacket. Keep hats and gloves with your coat.

Take out your books and homework from your backpack. Keep all other toys or games in your backpack.

Walk to your classroom and sit down at your desk. Talk quietly to your friends until the teacher starts class.

Arriving early to school will give you enough time to do all of these things and get a head start on your day.

Study Questions
Starting School in the Morning 4

Name _____ Date _____

Directions: Circle the answer.

1. When the bell rings:

    a. use your card and check out a book.

    b. check yourself and your backpack.

    c. walk quietly to your locker or coat rack.

2. What do you need to get out of your backpack?

    a. books and homework.

    b. lunch and tray.

    c. tickets and tokens.

Directions: Write the word to complete the sentence.

3. Walk to your classroom and sit down at your _____ .

　　　　　　　　　　　　　　　　　　　　　　　　　　(desk)

Challenge: Answer.

4. What should you leave in your backpack?

_____

5. Write one of your classroom rules.

_____

_____

The IMC is a place to find books to read, do research, or work on class projects.

You must use a quiet voice when speaking so you do not disturb others in the IMC.

The IMC 2

Ask the librarian if you need help finding books or other materials.

Use your IMC card to check out books.

The IMC 3

Listen to and follow the instructions from your teacher if you are with your class. Sit quietly at tables until it is time to leave.

Following these simple rules will make the IMC enjoyable for everyone.

Study Questions The IMC 4

Name _____ Date _____

Directions: Circle the answer.

1. The IMC is a good place to:

    a. eat or talk to friends.

    b. find books or work on class projects.

    c. scan pictures or do art work.

2. Who can help you find a book?

    a. a veterinarian.

    b. a clerk.

    c. a librarian.

Directions: Write the word to finish the sentence.

3. To check out a book, you need to have an IMC _____.

                                                     (card)

Challenge: Answer.

4. List three things you can do in your school IMC.

    a. _____

    b. _____

    c. _____

5. What is your favorite part of the IMC?

_____

The Lunchroom 1

Lunch is a time when you can see and talk to your friends while you eat. When you are in the lunchroom, use your classroom voice.

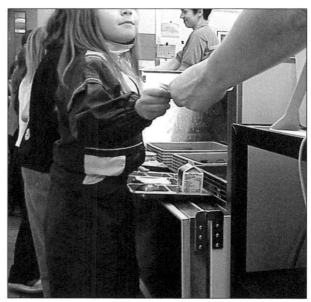

If you get food from the cafeteria line you need to have your lunch card ready. Wait in line until it is your turn to be served.

Carry your lunch to a table and sit down. Keep your hands to yourself while you eat.

Throw any trash away in the garbage cans when you are finished eating and return trays and utensils.

Wait for the lunchroom assistant to dismiss you.

Lunchtime is a fun time to be with your friends if you follow the lunchroom rules.

Study Questions **The Lunchroom** 4

Name _____ Date _____

Directions: Circle the answer.

1. What kind of voice should you use in the lunchroom?

    a. a quiet voice.

    b. a classroom voice.

    c. a playground voice.

2. What do you need to do when you're done eating?

    a. Give your lunch card to the cashier.

    b. Carry your food to a table.

    c. Put all the trash in the garbage cans.

Directions: Write the word to complete the sentence.

3. The lunchroom assistant dismisses you from the

_____.

(lunchroom)

Challenge: Answer.

4. What is one rule you must follow in your school lunchroom?

_____

5. What is your favorite lunchroom meal?

_____

Whether you are riding a bike or walking, there are many signs that you need to obey in the city.

If you ride a bike, you obey the same traffic signs as cars. Stop completely at stop signs and stop lights.

Some traffic signals tell you when and when not to cross the street.

Look for School Crossing signs near your school. They tell you where to cross the street.

City Signs 3

If you take a city bus, look for the bus stop signs.
They tell you where the bus will stop to pick you up.

Orange signs warn you about construction zones.

City Signs 4

Be careful in these areas and take a different route when the road or sidewalk is closed.

Railroad crossings are dangerous.

Life Skill Readers • Signs • **City Signs**

Some railroad crossings have gates with red flashing lights that block the road when a train comes.

Be aware of the signs around your city and obey them to stay safe.

Study Questions City Signs 6

Name _____ Date _____

Directions: Circle the answer.

1. Bike riders must obey what kind of signs?

    a. traffic signs.

    b. construction signs.

    c. city bus signs.

2. What do city bus signs tell you?

    a. when a train is coming.

    b. where the bus stops.

    c. where to cross for school.

Directions: Write the word to complete the sentence.

3. This sign means there is a _____ crossing.

    (railroad)

Challenge: Answer.

4. What do city signs help you to do?

    _____

5. What does this sign mean?

    _____

There are many different signs in the community. Signs give us important information. Some are for your safety and others help you find your way around.

Some signs look different but give the same information. Both signs show the location of a woman's restroom.

Other signs always look the same.

Some signs may have pictures or symbols on them,
while others are written.

Some signs combine pictures or symbols with words.

Everywhere you look you will find signs.

Study Questions
Community Signs 6

Name _____ Date _____

Directions: Circle the answer.

1. Community signs give you:

    a. information.

    b. tickets.

    c. transportation.

2. Community signs have either:

    a. bright colors or tickets.

    b. seatbelts or buttons.

    c. pictures or symbols.

Directions: Write the word to complete the sentence.

3. Everywhere you look you will find _____ .

    (signs)

Challenge: Answer.

4. What is one sign you see on your way to school?

_____

5. List three signs you see in your school.

    a. _____

    b. _____

    c. _____

Safety signs are everywhere. They have bright colors like red and yellow so we see them and pay attention.

Some have important words like Danger, Warning or Caution.

Often signs are to used protect us from things that are dangerous.

Others tell us where to go to stay safe.

Safety Signs 3

Some remind us to be careful.

Stay safe! Find, read and obey the safety signs you see.

Study Questions **Safety Signs 6**

Name _____ Date _____

Directions: Circle the answer.

1. Safety signs often have:

    a. bright colors or important words.

    b. tell where a bus stops.

    c. traffic information.

2. What do caution signs tell you?

    a. to use a seatbelt.

    b. to be careful.

    c. to watch traffic.

Directions: Write the word to complete the sentence.

3. Safety signs help you to stay _____.

                                               (safe)

Challenge: Answer.

4. What does a High Voltage sign mean?

_____

5. Where are safety signs in your school?

_____

Riding in a Car 1

If you are riding in a car it is important for you to think about safety.

When you get into a car, the first thing to do is put on the seat belt.

Riding in a Car 2

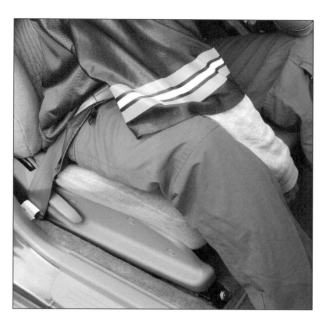
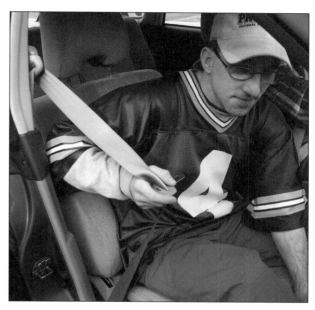

If your seat is uncomfortable, you can adjust it or ask the driver to help you adjust it.

There are many controls in the front seat.

If you are riding in the front seat, do not play with the controls.

It is polite to ask other people in the car before using the radio. Keep the volume low so it does not disturb the driver.

Some cars have windows that raise and lower by touching a button. Other windows use handles that turn.

When the car is moving do not stick arms or legs out the window.

Follow these rules when riding in a car and you will have a safe ride.

Study Questions **Riding in a Car** 6

Name _____ Date _____

Directions: Circle the answer.

1. When riding in a car always wear a:

   a. radio.

   b. seatbelt.

   c. hat.

2. One safety tip is to:

   a. play with the controls.

   b. play the radio loud.

   c. keep arms and legs inside the car.

Directions: Write the word to complete the sentence.

3. When riding in a car, do not distract the _____ .

                                              (driver)

Challenge: Answer.

4. Write one rule your family has about riding in a car.

   _____

5. Write one thing you learned about riding in a car.

   _____

Getting Around Town 1

There are many ways to travel around your town. How you get there depends on how far you are going.

Some people ride bikes when they go short distances like to work or school. Riding a bike is also a good way to get exercise.

Many people own cars. Cars are a good way to travel long distances.

A taxi is a special kind of car with its own driver. People use taxis to take them places they want to go.

Riding in taxis costs money. When the taxi arrives where you are going, you pay the driver. The farther you go the more you pay.

Many people in large cities ride buses. Buses always go the same routes. Places you can off or on are called bus stops.

Getting Around Town 4

Bus riders pay when they get on. Most buses have a fare box inside the door to put your money or bus pass in when you enter.

Some large cities have subways. Subways are like trains that run below ground.

Passengers buy tickets or tokens before they enter the subway station and wait for the train to arrive before they get on.

Not all types of transportation are found in every city. How many types of transportation do you have in your community?

Study Questions
Getting Around Town 6

Name _____ Date _____

Directions: Circle the answer.

1. What are some ways to get around town?

 a. cars, taxis and buses.

 b. planes, ships and trains.

 c. traffic and safety signs.

2. What kind of transportation do you have to pay for?

 a. bikes and cars.

 b. taxis and buses.

 c. walking and swimming.

Directions: Write the word to complete the sentence.

3. A train that goes underground is called a _____.

 (subway)

Challenge: Answer.

List three kinds of transportation you have in your town.

 a. _____

 b. _____

 c. _____

How do you get around your town?

_____

There are many ways to travel long distances.

Some people drive cars when they travel. Others take special vehicles that they use only to travel long distances.

Traveling Long Distance 2

Some buses are designed to carry people on long trips. They have comfortable seats, a bathroom and storage space for luggage.

Trains are a fast way to travel. They make few stops and go faster than cars or buses.

Traveling Long Distance 3

Airplanes are another way to travel. They are the fastest way to travel long distances.

There are many different types of transportation.

Study Questions
Traveling Long Distance 4

Name _____ Date _____

Directions: Circle the answer.

1. One way to travel long distance is by:

    a. a car.

    b. a bike.

    c. walking.

2. A fast way to travel long distance is to use a:

    a. train.

    b. bike.

    c. walking path.

Directions: Write the word to complete the sentence.

3. The fastest way to travel is to go by _____.

                                          (plane)

Challenge: Answer.

4. What did you use to travel on a long trip?

_____

5. Where did you go?

_____

Product Engineer 1

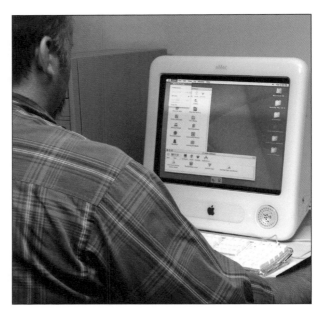

Don works at a company that makes computer software. One of Don's responsibilities is to test software for bugs. A bug is a problem in the software.

He tests the software on different computers to make sure it will work for everyone who uses it.

Product Engineer 2

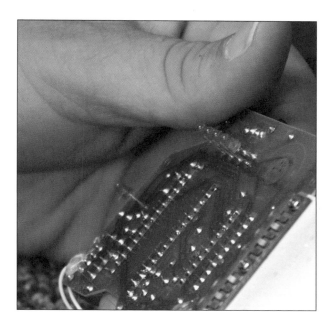

Inside electronic devices are tiny circuit boards. They carry electricity that makes the product work.

When products break, Don tests them with his tools. A meter tells him if the electricity is going where it should.

Product Engineer 3

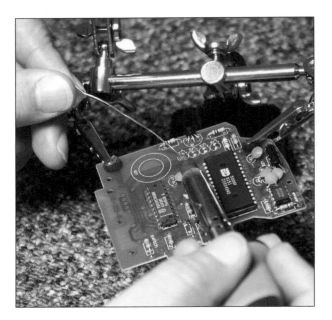 

A soldering iron is used to mend tiny electrical paths.
The iron is hot so he uses it carefully.

Don's job is important because he makes sure the
products are working well.

Name _____ Date _____

Directions: Circle the answer.

1. A bug in computer software is:

    a. an insect.

    b. a problem.

    c. a drawing tablet.

2. What are some tools a product engineer uses?

    a. meters and soldering irons.

    b. scanners and drawing tablets.

    c. ladders and forklifts.

Directions: Write the word to complete the sentence.

3. A person who fixes software and electronic devices is called a product _____.

                  (engineer)

Challenge: Answer.

4. Write one thing you learned about a product engineer.

_____

5. Would you like to be a product engineer?

      yes   no

Graphic Artist 1

Kevin is a graphic artist. His job is to design and draw the artwork for books and catalogs.

He uses a computer to help him design. A drawing tablet helps him draw pictures on the computer screen.

Graphic Artist 2

A scanner is used to put pictures from books in his computer so he can work on them.

When he is finished designing the art he prints it to make sure it looks good.

Graphic Artist 3

Kevin enjoys his job because he can draw new things everyday.

Study Questions **Graphic Artist** 4

Name _____ Date _____

Directions: Circle the answer.

1. What does a graphic artist do?

    a. fixes electronic devices and computer software.

    b. uses spreadsheets and database programs.

    c. draws for books and catalogs.

2. What are some tools a graphic artist uses?

    a. drawing tablets and computers.

    b. ladders and forklifts.

    c. spreadsheets and database programs.

Directions: Write the word to complete the sentence.

3. A person who draws for books and catalogs is a graphic

_____.

(artist)

Challenge: Answer.

4. What do you need to know to become a graphic artist?

_____

5. Is this a job you would like to do?

    yes   no

Working in a Warehouse 1

Lindsay works in a warehouse for a large company.

A warehouse is where they keep products to sell to customers.
It has rows of shelves that store products.

Working in a Warehouse 2

Lindsay uses a computer to print orders from customers. The orders tell her what products she needs to take off the shelves.

She is careful when using a ladder or forklift to reach products that are on the top shelves.

Then, she puts the products the customers ordered into a box and fills it with packing material so it does not break.

Then she seals the box with tape.

Working in a Warehouse 4

Next, she weighs the box and puts an address label on it.

At the end of the day, a driver picks up all the boxes to be sent to the customers.

Working in a warehouse is a lot of fun but it takes a lot of energy.

Study Questions
Working in a Warehouse 6

Name _____ Date _____

Directions: Circle the answer.

1. What does a warehouse worker do?

    a. makes reports that show company sales.

    b. fixes computer software.

    c. prints and ships customer orders.

2. What tools does a warehouse worker use?

    a. ladders, forklifts and computers.

    b. drawing tablets and computers.

    c. meters and soldering irons.

Directions: Write the word to compete the sentence.

3. A person who ships orders to customers is

a _____ worker.

    (warehouse)

Challenge: Answer.

4. Write one thing a warehouse worker does.

_____

5. What do you think you need to know before becoming a

warehouse worker?

_____

Susan is a manager at a small company. She makes sure other workers in the company do their jobs right.

A computer at her desk helps her with her work.

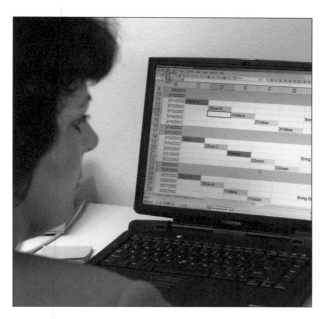

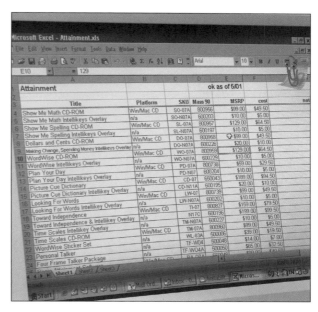

Spreadsheet and database programs keep track of inventory in the warehouse. Inventory means products the company sells.

Susan uses the computer to print reports that show how company sales are doing.

Good organization and communication skills are needed to be a manager.

Study Questions
Working in an Office 4

Name _____ Date _____

Directions: Circle the answer.

1. What does a company manager do?

    a. keeps track of sales and workers.

    b. keeps track of electronic devices.

    c. keeps track of orders from customers.

2. What are some tools a company manager use?

    a. ladders and fork lifts.

    b. meters and soldering irons.

    c. spreadsheets and database programs.

Directions: Write the word to complete the sentence.

3. _____ means products a company sells.

    (Inventory)

Challenge: Answer.

4. What kind of skills does a company manger need to have?

    a. _____

    b. _____

5. What do you think you would need to know before becoming a company manager?

    _____